Saint Joseph

Book of Prayers
for Children

By
FATHER LAWRENCE G. LOVASIK, S.V.D.

CATHOLIC BOOK PUBLISHING CORPORATION
NEW JERSEY

Presented
to

From

date

NIHIL OBSTAT: Francis J. McAree, S.T.D.   *Censor Librorum*
IMPIMATUR: ✛ Patrick J. Sheridan, D.D.
Vicar General, Archdiocese of New York

(T-148)

Printed in Hong Kong   ISBN 978-0-89942-148-3

CONTENTS

When we pray, we raise our hearts and minds to God. We talk to God: Father, Son, and Holy Spirit. We adore God as Our Creator. We give Him thanks for all His blessings. We beg His forgiveness for our faults. We ask for His help in our daily lives. We can also pray to Mary, the Mother of Jesus and to the Saints who had great love for Jesus. They will ask God to help us.

The Glory Be

Glory be to the Father,
and to the Son,
and to the Holy Spirit.
As it was in the beginning,
is now, and ever shall be,
world without end.
Amen.

Morning Prayer

My heavenly Father,
I thank You for this new day.
May I live it all for You
as Your good and loving child.

I know that You watch over me,
and love me in everything You send.

Little Prayers during the Day

Dear Jesus, help me to say
little prayers during the day.

Thanks be to God.

Lord, I love You.

Praised be Jesus Christ.

Lord Jesus, bless all the children of the world.

Holy Spirit, make my soul holy.

Holy Mary, pray for us.

O Mary conceived without sin, pray for us who have recourse to you.

Prayers before and after Meals

Bless us, O Lord,
and these Your gifts,
which we are about to receive
from Your goodness
through Christ our Lord.
Amen.

We give You thanks,
Almighty God,
for all Your gifts,
which we have received
through Christ our Lord.
Amen.

11

Night Prayer

I thank You, Lord,
for having been with me all this day.
I thank You for the many good things
You have done for me.

I ask you to forgive me
for anything I have done wrong.
I know that You love me all the more
if I am truly sorry.

Bless my dear mother and father
and my brothers and sisters,
and all those who are kind to me.
Help us all to love You more
and serve You well tomorrow.

Prayer to God the Father

Heavenly Father, I thank You
for the life You gave me
and for all the things You do
to make me happy in this world.
I thank You for the stars and sky,
for the hills and fields and lakes,
for flowers, trees, and grass,
for birds and all animals.

14

Never let me forget
Your love for me.
I give You all my love
and all that I do.

Prayer to God the Son

Jesus, I believe that You are my Lord
and my Savior,
the Redeemer of the human race,
Who died on the Cross
for the salvation of all people,
and Who died also for me.

I thank You
for having opened heaven
to me
by Your death on the Cross.

Without You I cannot save my soul.
As You gave Your life for me,
may I always live my life for You.

Prayer to God the Holy Spirit

Holy Spirit, my God,
the Third Person
of the Blessed Trinity,
I love You.

I thank You for the grace
You have given me
to make my soul beautiful
and to help me to be good.

Your grace made me a child of God;
it opened heaven to me.

Holy Spirit, live in my soul
and take me to heaven someday.

Prayers to Mary Our Mother

I want to love you
as Jesus did.
I give myself to you
that you may protect me
and guide me to Jesus
your Son.

I pray to you in these words:

Hail Mary, full of grace!
The Lord is with you;
blessed are you among women,
and blessed is the fruit
of your womb, Jesus.

Holy Mary, Mother of God,
pray for us sinners,
now, and at the hour
of our death.
Amen.

Prayer to My Patron Saint

Dear Saint . . . .
I have been honored to bear your name,
which you made famous by your holiness.
Help me never to shame this name.

Obtain God's grace for me
that I may grow in faith, hope, and love
and all the virtues.

Watch over me all my life
and bring me safe to my heavenly home.

Prayer to My Guardian Angel

Angel of God,
my Guardian dear,
God's love for me
has sent you here.

Ever this day
be at my side,
to light and guard,
to rule and guide.

Keep me from all danger,
and lead me to heaven.

Prayer for My Family

Dear Jesus, I thank You
for the good
mother and father
You gave me.

I thank You
for my brothers and sisters,
for my home,
for my food and clothes,
and for all the good
things I receive.

Bless my parents
for all they do for me.
Give them grace and health
now on earth.

Prayer for My Relatives

Dear Jesus,
You have also given me relatives,
grandparents, aunts and uncles,
and cousins my own age.

When our families get together,
we always have fun,
playing games and laughing a lot.

They are part of my family,
my "extended" family;
help me to be good to them
and make them happy.

Prayer for My Friends

Jesus, You love children;
You laid Your hands on them in prayer and
   blessed them.
You said, "Let the children come to Me."

Help us to be kind to each other
as You always were.
When I work or study or play with my friends
may I always be good to them.
Keep us from all that is bad
that we may all be Your friends.

Prayer for My Teachers

Jesus, Your Mother Mary
and good Saint Joseph were Your teachers
when You were a child like me.

Help me always to study hard
to please my parents and teachers,
but especially to please You.

Jesus, bless my teachers
who work so hard for me.

Prayer for Those Who Teach Us Religion

Dear Lord,
bless our Holy Father, our bishops and priests,
who take Your place among us.
They teach us Your truth, take away our sins,
and offer Holy Mass.

Bless all those who teach us
to know and love You.
Reward them in heaven.

Prayer for Those Who Help Us

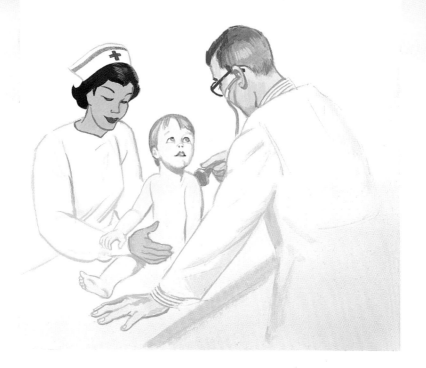

Heavenly Father, I thank You
for all the people
who help us;
doctors, nurses, policemen,
firemen, and many other working people.

Help me to be kind to them
and to pray for them.

Prayer for Sunday Blessings

Dear Lord,
Sunday is a special day,
the day of the Lord—
Father, Son, and Holy Spirit.
It is set aside
for us to thank and praise You,
especially at Holy Mass.

Help me to rest
from the usual things I do
and think about God.
May everyone in my family be happy,
and let us be good to other people.

Prayer for Weekday Blessings

Dear Lord,
this day is a gift from You;
let me make good use of it.

Help me to do what I have to do
so that I may grow
in body, mind, and soul.

Prayer before Going to Confession

Sometimes we speak to God because we did something wrong and we want to ask His forgiveness; that is why we go to confession. We tell our sins to the priest and he offers God's own forgiveness. Other times we ask God's forgiveness in our heart while we are at home, or in school, or wherever we are. We know that God will listen to us until we get a chance to go to confession. One of the prayers we can use to ask God's forgiveness is:

Jesus, my Lord and my God,
I am sorry for all my sins
because they have offended You.
You died on the Cross
because of my sins.
I want to try hard
to keep away from sin
so that I may always be Your friend
and to show You that I really love You.

J esus, I believe that at the Last Supper
You gave the Holy Eucharist,
the sacrifice of Your Body and Blood,
to continue for all time
the sacrifice of the Cross.

Prayer before Mass and Communion

The priest at Mass,
by the power he receives from You,
really brings You on the altar
and offers You to God the Father,
in the name of all the people.

Prayer before the Blessed Sacrament

Jesus I thank You
for staying in the Tabernacle
day and night to be with me
and hear my prayers
when I need Your help.

You are my best Friend.
I want to come to visit You often.

O Sacrament most Holy,
O Sacrament Divine,
all praise and all thanksgiving
be ev'ry moment Thine!

The Our Father

One day the disciples were listening to Jesus teach, and when He had finished they asked Him a favor. They had heard all sorts of prayers, and they wanted Jesus to teach them a special prayer that God would really like. Jesus taught them that we should all call God our Father because He loves us as His very own children. He then taught the disciples, and us, to pray to God, our Father, as follows:

Our Father,
Who art in heaven,
hallowed be Thy Name.
Thy kingdom come,
Thy will be done on earth as it is in heaven.

Give us this day our daily bread,
and forgive us our trespasses
as we forgive those who trespass against us.

And lead us not into temptation,
but deliver us from evil.

49

Prayer of Thanks on Receiving Toys

Dear Jesus,
I thank You for the toys.

When You were a Child
I am sure that You also had toys.

I know that many children in the world
are poor, and have no toys to play with.
Please, help all those children.

Help me to thank my parents for the nice things they buy for me by praying for them.

Prayer of Thanks for All Good Things

Let me learn from the good things
that I see and hear,
but keep me from watching
whatever may harm my soul.

Teach me how to enjoy
Your many gifts
and use them to help me
love You more
and serve You better.

Prayer of Thanks for the Bible and Prayer Books

Heavenly Lord,
thank You for giving us the Bible,
which is the Word of God.

Thank You also for the Prayer Books, which help us learn to speak to You and also tell us about Your Church and her teachings.

Prayer of Thanks for My Pets

Jesus, I thank You for the many things
You give me that make my life happy.
You give me the little animals
to be my companions.
They remind me
of how much You care for me.

I want to be kind to my pets
and to all animals
because You made them
to give You glory.

Prayer of Thanks for the World

Heavenly Father, I thank You
for the life You gave me
and for all the things You do
to make me happy in this world.

I thank You for the stars and sky,
for hills and fields, and lakes,
for flowers, trees, and grass,
for birds, and all the animals.

Never let me forget
that I belong to You
and that You want all my love.
Heaven—which is more beautiful
than all this world of nature—
is waiting for me.

Prayer of Thanks for My Country

Lord, thank You
for letting me be free
to live in peace
and to worship You
without fear.

IN GOD
WE TRUST

Watch over our leaders
in government, and help them
to make just laws.

Help all the citizens of our Country
to follow Your holy Will
and to live in love for each other
and for You.

Prayer of Thanks for Each Day

Dear Jesus, I thank You,
for each day of my life is a gift from You.
Help me to use it well,
to serve You and the people I meet each day.
Thank You for each birthday
that makes me think
of Your love for me.

Prayer for Needy Children

Lord, there are many children
who do not have a home
because they are too poor.
Some are homeless and lonesome
because they have no parents,
or have lost their home
because of war, or floods,
or earthquakes . . . .

Lord, please help
all those children
and all people
who need a home
and food
and clothes—
and hope.